50
GREATEST HITS

THE
CONNOR TIFARRA
COLLECTION

50
GREATEST HITS

THE
CONNOR TIFARRA
COLLECTION

CONNOR TIFARRA

50 Greatest Hits The Connor Tifarra Collection
Copyright © 2015 Connor Tifarra,
Connor Tifarra Entertainment
All rights reserved. No part of this book may be reproduced in any form or by any electronic or mechanical means including information storage and retrieval systems without permission in writing from the author or publisher, except by a reviewer who may quote brief passages in a review. All songs, words and music are written by and copyrighted by Connor Tifarra and Connor Tifarra Entertainment. Published by, Connor Tifarra and Connor Tifarra Entertainment.

First Edition
Copyright © 2015 Connor Tifarra,
Connor Tifarra Entertainment

All rights reserved

ISBN-10: 0692493050

ISBN-13: 978-0692493052

For Theresa and Sasha

CONTENTS

The Songs

Love Is What She Wants   1
Such A Beautiful Girl   4
We're In Love With Each Other   6
She's A Country Lady   9
A Rock 'n Roll Girl   12
Love Me   14
Back To Back   17
Straight To Your Heart   22
Sometimes You Win, Sometimes You Lose   25
Key To My Heart   27
Rollin' On Down The Line   29
They Call Me A Rebel   31
40 Long Days   34

It's Been A Good Life   37
I Tripped And Fell In Love   40
Yesterday Was A Damn Good Day   43
Broken Promises   46
Nothing Lasts   49
Let's Fly Away   51
Two Young Lovers   53
Next Time You're Lonely   55
Watching The Wagon Wheel Roll 'Round   58
The Brave   60
Rainy Day Girl   62
You're My Rainy Day Girl   65
21 Lovers Lane   68
Letting Go of Love   71
Roses, Rainbows And You   73
Looking At The Outside   75
Holly   77
Time Plays The Game   79
Trapped   82
Turn My Life Around   85
Delusions   87
I'm Feeling Down   89
I'll Have To Dream Alone   91
The Decision   94
Exit 41   97
Invisible   100
Expensive Bitch   103

All My Life   106
Heart of Fire   109
TIC-TAC-DIE   111
Undercover Lies   114
The American Dream   118
Defenestration   122
Countdown Clock   126
Better Go Get Her   129
I'm Coming Home For Christmas   132
The New Year Is Here   134

About The Songs

Introduction   139

Love Is What She Wants, Such A Beautiful Girl   141

We're In Love With Each Other   142

She's A Country Lady, A Rock 'n Roll Girl   143

Love Me, Back To Back, Straight To Your Heart   144

Sometimes You Win, Sometimes You Lose, Key To My Heart, Rollin' On Down The Line, They Call Me A Rebel, 40 Long Days   145

It's Been A Good Life, I Tripped And Fell In Love, Yesterday Was A Damn Good Day   146

Broken Promises   147

Nothing Lasts, Let's Fly Away, Two Young Lovers, Next Time You're Lonely   148

Watching The Wagon Wheel Roll 'Round, The Brave, Rainy Day Girl, You're My Rainy Day Girl   149

21 Lovers Lane, Letting Go of Love, Roses, Rainbows And You   150

Looking At The Outside, Holly, Time Plays The Game   151

Trapped, Turn My Life Around, Delusions, I'm Feeling Down, I'll Have To Dream Alone, The Decision, Exit 41   152

Invisible, Expensive Bitch   153

All My Life, Heart of Fire, TIC-TAC-DIE   154

Undercover Lies, The American Dream   155

Defenestration, Countdown Clock, Better Go Get Her   156

I'm Coming Home For Christmas, The New Year Is Here   157

50 GREATEST HITS

THE
CONNOR TIFARRA
COLLECTION

THE SONGS

LOVE IS WHAT SHE WANTS

© 2005 Connor Tifarra, Connor Tifarra Entertainment

This girl's all alone
She doesn't want it that way
She'd love to settle down and have a family someday
She's always wanted someone
To treat her like a queen
So far, that's still a dream

Loneliness can hurt
Life can seem so tough
When there's no one to love you
And you want to be loved

Dreams can fall apart
Just as fast as they came
She doesn't understand it
She's not to blame

All she wants is to be in love
She's been alone for long enough
Reaching a dream can seem so tough
But she's never giving up

Love is what she wants
Love is what she needs
Love will win her heart
Love is what it takes
Love is what she wants

Love is what she needs
If you want to know this girl
Give her all the love that she needs

She has a heart of gold
She's not too bold
She's a little shy until she meets the right guy
She loves to sing and dance
She really wants the chance
To show someone who she is inside

But her dreams still linger on
This girl is still all alone
How long will this go on?
She hopes it not too long
With this girl you can't go wrong
Love is what she wants

She's always dreamed of being in love
She's been alone for long enough
Reaching a dream can seem so tough
But she's never giving up

Love is what she wants
Love is what she needs
Love will win her heart
Love is what it takes
Love is what she wants
Love is what she needs
If you want to know this girl
Give her all the love that she needs

Love is what she wants
Love is what she needs

Love is what she wants
Love is what she needs

Love is what she wants
Love is what she needs

Love is what she wants
Love is what she needs

LOVE IS WHAT SHE WANTS
© 2005 Connor Tifarra, Connor Tifarra Entertainment

SUCH A BEAUTIFUL GIRL

© 2004 Connor Tifarra, Connor Tifarra Entertainment

I went out late last night
Hoping to catch the sight of a beautiful girl
I went to my favorite club called The Little White Dove
Just down the hill

When I walked into the room I could smell her perfume
She was sitting at a table all alone, I couldn't help but stare
I looked into her eyes then she took me by surprise
When she waived come over here

Then she took me by the hand
Straight to the dance floor we ran

And we danced all night long while the band played her favorite love songs
We laughed and talked
How we carried on
I was lucky last night
To catch the sight of a beautiful girl
Such a beautiful girl

Her hair smelled like roses
When I held her close and we danced cheek to cheek
Her eyes were hypnotizing, her lips were so inviting
That I could hardly speak

Then she put her lips to mine

I almost lost my mind

Yeah we danced all night long while the band played her favorite love songs
We laughed and talked
How we carried on
I was lucky last night
To catch the sight of a beautiful girl
Such a beautiful girl

I wonder if I'm ever going to see her again
Or smell her perfume in the summer wind
I can't pretend
She was out of this world
She was such a beautiful girl

Yeah we danced all night long while the band played her favorite love songs
We laughed and talked
Oh how we carried on
I was lucky last night
To catch the sight of a beautiful girl
Such a beautiful girl

I was lucky last night
I caught the sight of a beautiful girl
Such a beautiful girl
She was such a beautiful girl

SUCH A BEAUTIFUL GIRL
© 2004 Connor Tifarra, Connor Tifarra Entertainment

WE'RE IN LOVE WITH EACH OTHER

© 2015 Connor Tifarra, Connor Tifarra Entertainment

She's something special
She's everything I need
She makes life blissful
From front to back and in between

Every time she kisses me
I feel the beating of my heart
When she's lying next to me
I know what we are

We're in love with each other
I'm just right for her
She's perfect for me
We're in love with each other
We fit together perfectly
We're so happy
Our love comes naturally
I love her and she loves me

She loves the moonlight
And root beer floats on a rainy night
She makes me thankful
She fills my heart with delight

Every time she kisses me
I feel the beating of my heart

When she's lying next to me
I know what we are

We're in love with each other
I'm just right for her
She's perfect for me
We're in love with each other
We fit together perfectly
We're so happy
Our love comes naturally
I love her and she loves me

She knows I love her
I say it to her everyday
She's sweet like nectar
Like a hummingbird we fly away

Every time we kiss
We feel the beating of our hearts
When she's lying next to me
We both know what we are

We're in love with each other
I'm just right for her
She's perfect for me
We're in love with each other
We fit together perfectly
We so happy
Our love comes naturally

We're in love with each other
I'm just right for her

She's perfect for me
We're in love with each other
We fit together perfectly
We so happy
Our love comes naturally
I love her and she loves me

(Yeah she loves me)
She loves me
(I know she does)
She loves me
(She knows that I love her)
She loves me
(I'm always thinking of her)
She loves me
(Yeah I love her)
And she loves me

SHE'S A COUNTRY LADY

© 2007 Connor Tifarra, Connor Tifarra Entertainment

She lives in the city
That's not where she wants to be
She looks so pretty
She wants to trade her suit for blue jeans

She's tired of city life
There's too much strife
She wants to slow down
She's got to get out of town

She's a country lady
She has dreams of leaving the big city
Something's got to change
She's got to find a way
Deep in her heart she knows
She's a country lady

She's always wanted
A place where she can make an escape
She's always needed
To feel a soft and sweet country breeze

She wants to walk around
With bare feet on the ground
She needs to slow down
She's got to get out of town

She's a country lady
She has dreams of leaving the big city
Something's got to change
She's got to find a way
Deep in her heart she knows
She's a country lady

She's lived in the city all of her life
She hasn't seen the stars on a clear warm night
She's only seen the city lights
And dreaming of country nights

She works in the city
That's not where she wants to be
She's a southern beauty
Making plans for her getaway

She's tired of city life
There's too much strife
She wants to slow down
She's got to get out of town

She's a country lady
She has dreams of leaving the big city
Something's got to change
She's got to find a way
Deep in her heart she knows
She's a country lady

She's a country lady
She has dreams of leaving the big city
Something's got to change

She's got to find a way
Deep in her heart she knows
She's a country lady

SHE'S A COUNTRY LADY
© 2007 Connor Tifarra, Connor Tifarra Entertainment

A ROCK 'n ROLL GIRL

© 2004 Connor Tifarra, Connor Tifarra Entertainment

She's new in town
She's tired of sittin' around
Goin' out tonight gonna paint the town
She wants to rock 'n roll and have some fun
She headed out the door fast as a smokin' gun

She looked around the town for a place to rock
But she only found a country club on every block
She finally gave up and had to give in
She picked a country club and walked right on in

You should have seen the smile on every guys face
When this rock 'n roll chick stepped her foot in the place
She went straight to the jukebox put a dollar on in
That's when her change began

She thought she was gonna rock but she ended up
Kickin' up her heels to a new sound that she loved
Once she got that country music in her soul
She found she liked it more than her rock 'n roll
She use to be a rocker but she's had enough
She's a rock 'n roll girl in a country club

The jukebox started playin'
She was tappin' her feet
This rock 'n roll girl loved that country beat
Once she heard the music it went straight to her heart

She should have been a country girl right from the start

There ain't no turnin' back once you've had a taste
Good 'ol country music just can't be replaced
There ain't nothin' wrong with rock 'n roll
But a kickin' country song brings a chill to her bones

She thought she was gonna rock but she ended up
Kickin' up her heels to a new sound that she loved
Once she got that country music in her soul
She found she liked it more than her rock 'n roll
She use to be a rocker but she's had enough
She's a rock 'n roll girl in a country club

She thought she was gonna rock but she ended up
Kickin' up her heels to a new sound that she loved
Once she got that country music in her soul
She found she liked it more than her rock 'n roll
She use to be a rocker but she's had enough
She's a rock 'n roll girl in a country club

Yeah, she use to be a rock 'n roller but she's had enough
She's a rock 'n roll girl in a country club

A ROCK 'n ROLL GIRL
© 2004 Connor Tifarra, Connor Tifarra Entertainment

LOVE ME

© 2003 Connor Tifarra, Connor Tifarra Entertainment

Love me, c'mon and love me
Love me my baby or let me be
Love me, c'mon and love me
Love me my baby or set me free

You probably think I'm crazy for feeling this way
But I've been thinking 'bout you baby night and day
No other woman could treat you so good
You won't be sorry 'cuz my lovin' is so good

I don't know how many girls said I love you
But they couldn't love you like me
C'mon baby put your arms around me
I want to love you for eternity

Love me, c'mon and love me
Love me my baby or let me be
Love me, c'mon and love me
Love me my baby or set me free

I've been watching you from afar
I feel like a school girl chasing a movie star
I want to kiss your lips and feel your touch
Run my fingers through your hair
Make you want me so much

I don't know how many girls said I love you

But they couldn't love you like me
C'mon baby put your arms around me
I want to love you for eternity

Love me, c'mon and love me
Love me my baby or let me be
Love me, c'mon and love me
Love me my baby or set me free

You drive me out of my mind
You're always lookin' so fine
I love the way you walk
I love the way you talk
C'mon and love me all time
Baby be mine

I would love you baby like no other girl could
I'm a one man woman, my lovin' is so good
C'mon baby won't you hold me real tight
Make love with me every day and night

I don't know how many girls said I love you
But they couldn't love you like me
C'mon baby put your arms around me
I want to love you for eternity

Love me, c'mon and love me
Love me my baby or let me be
Love me, c'mon and love me
Love me my baby or set me free

Love me

Love me

Love me
(You know that I want you)
Love me
(You know that I need you)
Love me
(Wrap my arms around you)

Love me
Love me

Love me
C'mon and love me

Love me
C'mon and love me

Love me
C'mon and love me

Love me
C'mon and love me

Love me

LOVE ME
© 2003 Connor Tifarra, Connor Tifarra Entertainment

BACK TO BACK

© 2015 Connor Tifarra, Connor Tifarra Entertainment

Here comes the night
Another sleepless night
I'm so tired of fighting
Tired of hiding

Neither one of us wants to be the first
To say I'm sorry
Now back to back we lay

The night seems so long
When no one admits their wrong
And you can't close your eyes

Silence fills the room
The quiet sets the mood
Two hearts are aching

Here comes the night
Another sleepless night
Two hearts gone astray
We'll try to find our way
In a new days light

Neither one of us wants to be the first
To carry the weight
Or say any words
Neither one of us

Has the courage to say I'm sorry
Back to back we lay

No dreaming tonight
On this sleepless night
We're both tired of fighting
Tired of lying

Thinking about the day
And what you're going to say
But you won't say goodnight

Two hearts turn away
Blue skies turn to grey
Here comes the moonlight

Here comes the night
Another sleepless night
Two hearts on the mend
Try starting again
In a new days light

Neither one of us wants to be the first
To break the ice
Or speak any words
Neither one of us can sleep tonight
We'll both be awake
'Till the morning light

Holding back tears
Both hurting inside
We're both tired of fighting

Tired of trying

We both face the wall
No relief in sight at all
Two hearts are breaking

Here comes the night
Another sleepless night
Two hearts gone astray
We'll try to find our way
In a new days light

Neither one of us wants to be the first
To carry the weight
Or say any words
Neither one of us
Has the courage to say I'm sorry
Back to back we lay

Our eyes open wide
Back to back
Trying our best to hide

No hope in sight
It's going to be a sleepless night

Two lives gone astray
Will we move on and forget today?

Back to back we lay
Each facing our own way
Two hearts are frozen

Our love is broken

Here comes the night
Another sleepless night
I'm so tired of fighting
Tired of hiding

Neither one of us wants to be the first
To say I'm sorry
Back to back we lay

Neither one of us
Has the courage to say I love you
Back to back we lay

Neither one of us wants to be the first
To say I'm sorry
Back to back we lay

Neither one of us
Has the courage to say I love you
Back to back we lay

Neither one of us wants to be the first
To say I'm sorry
Back to back we lay

Neither one of us
Has the courage to say I love you
Back to back we lay

Neither one of us wants to be the first

To say I'm sorry
Back to back we lay

Neither one of us
Has the courage to say I love you

STRAIGHT TO YOUR HEART

© 2005 Connor Tifarra, Connor Tifarra Entertainment

It's hard on a soldier
When they have to go away
Defenders of freedom
Helping the world see a brighter day

Don't worry about me
I'm doing ok
I'll be home soon
I can't wait for that day

All my love is in every word I write
All my love is in my prayers each night
So don't be afraid
Don't cry a tear
I'll be home soon dear
Until then,

Straight to your heart
I'm sending my love
Straight to your heart
On the wings of a dove
And it won't be long
'Till I come home
I'm sending my love to your heart

Fighting for freedom
No one should have to do

Freedom should come easy
From my point of view

Some people live in the dark
They can't see any light
Instead of living a good life
We're watching people die

I don't know why the world has to be this way
I don't know why peace is so hard
But I'm not afraid
Don't cry a tear
I'll be home soon dear
Until then,

Straight to your heart
I'm sending my love
Straight to your heart
On the wings of a dove
And it won't be long
'Till I come home
I'm sending my love to your heart

I hope and pray
This war will be over soon
Then I'll be on a plane
Coming home to you

I'll hold you in my arms
I'll feel your touch again
Don't be afraid
No need for tears

I'll be home soon dear
Until then,

Straight to your heart
I'm sending my love
Straight to your heart
On the wings of a dove
And it won't be long
'Till I come home
I'm sending my love to your heart

No it won't be long
'Till I come home
I'm sending my love to your heart

STRAIGHT TO YOUR HEART
© 2005 Connor Tifarra, Connor Tifarra Entertainment

SOMETIMES YOU WIN, SOMETIMES YOU LOSE

© 2005 Connor Tifarra, Connor Tifarra Entertainment

(3 voice harmony a cappella intro)
Sometimes you win
Sometimes you lose
Sometimes you smile
Sometimes you get the blues

Sometimes you win
Sometimes you lose
In each and everything you do
There's a choice that you have to make
Don't you give up no matter what it takes

You can stay on that road
But where will it lead?
A new direction may be what you need

You can sit at the crossroads wondering which way to turn
Where will you go?
What will you learn?

No matter which road you choose
Sometimes you win
Sometimes you lose

If you give up who knows what could have been
Reach for the top

Don't ever give in

Sometimes a dream can seem hard to reach
Dreams can come true
If you just believe

Whichever road you choose
Sometimes you win
Sometimes you lose

Always reach for the stars
Always follow your heart
Do it for you
Do what you've got to do
Make your wish come true

Everything will be just fine
Sometimes it takes a little more time
Sometimes you win
Sometimes you lose
Sometimes you smile
Sometimes you get the blues

SOMETIMES YOU WIN, SOMETIMES YOU LOSE
© 2005 Connor Tifarra, Connor Tifarra Entertainment

KEY TO MY HEART

© 2006 Connor Tifarra, Connor Tifarra Entertainment

You own the key to my heart
My love belongs to you
I knew it right from the start
When you unlocked my heart
That I would give it to you

I never felt like this
All it took was your kiss
You had my heart doing flips
I've been living in bliss
Since I fell in love

I've never felt a love this strong
I know it can't be wrong
My heart's been locked up inside me for so long
There's no need to hide it
I'm so excited
It's a love I never knew
I'm so in love with you

You own the key to my heart
My love belongs to you
I knew it right from the start
When you unlocked my heart
That I would give it to you

My heart's been broke a few times

That was enough for me
It's been torn all apart
I put a lock on my heart
And hid the key

It's one of a kind
It can't be replaced
You can't duplicate this key
There's only one of me
And one key to my heart

I've never felt a love this strong
I know it can't be wrong
My heart chose you to love all my life long
There's no need to hide it
I'm so excited
It's a love that's all brand new
I'm so in love with you

You own the key to my heart
My love belongs to you
I knew it right from the start
When you unlocked my heart
That I would give it to you

I knew it right from the start
When you unlocked my heart
That I would give it to you

KEY TO MY HEART
© 2006 Connor Tifarra, Connor Tifarra Entertainment

ROLLIN' ON DOWN THE LINE

© 2003 Connor Tifarra, Connor Tifarra Entertainment

Rollin' on down the line
Can't find no reason or rhyme
When ya comin' back?
Am I on the right track?
Can you just give me a sign?

Rollin' on down the line
Don't want to waste any time
Got to find my baby
Rollin' on down the line

I went to Club Madeline's
To see if you were dancin' in line
But you weren't two steppin' there
Your boots were out dancin' somewhere

Rollin' on down the line
Don't want to waste any time
Got to find my baby
Rollin' on down the line

I went to the club Thunder Bay
And there you were dancin' away
I jumped in the line ~
Baby you were mine ~
Oh yeah baby you're dancin' so fine

Rollin' on down the line
I don't have waste no more time
'Cuz I found my baby
Rollin' on down the line

Rollin' on down the line
Rollin' on down the line
Rollin' on down the line
I don't have waste no more time
Me and my line dancin' baby
Are rollin' on down the line

Rollin' on down the line
Rollin' on down the line
Rollin' on down the line
Rollin' on down the line
Me and my line dancin' baby
Are rollin' on down the line

ROLLIN' ON DOWN THE LINE
© 2003 Connor Tifarra, Connor Tifarra Entertainment

THEY CALL ME A REBEL
© 2005 Connor Tifarra, Connor Tifarra Entertainment

Some people call me a rebel
They say I'm wild and crazy
The open road is what I know
Lovin' life
Ridin' free

I ride like the wind
Feelin' the breeze on my skin
Cruisin' on my bike
Back on the road again

My Harley's never let me down
She's taken me from town to town
From EK Loop in good old Butte
Out to Sturgis and Tennessee
Oh, I love the way she feels ridin' down the highway

Some people call me a rebel
They say I'm hell on two wheels
I ride with pride through the countryside
With leather boots
My mirrored shades

And I ride like the wind
Feelin' the breeze on my skin
Cruisin' on my bike
Back on the road again

My Harley's never let me down
She's taken me from town to town
From EK Loop in good old Butte
Out to Sturgis and Tennessee
Oh, I love the way she feels ridin' down the highway

I've got a front row view
Cruising up the avenue

Dressed to ride
My sunroof is the sky

I love to ride
It feels like I can fly

Some people call me a rebel
They say I'm wild and crazy
The open road is what I know
Lovin' life
Ridin' free

I ride like the wind
Feelin' the breeze on my skin
Cruisin' on my bike
Back on the road again

My Harley's never let me down
She's taken me from town to town
From EK Loop in good old Butte
Out to Sturgis and Tennessee
Oh, I love the way she feels ridin' down the highway
Ridin' down the highway

Ridin' down the highway

Ridin' down the highway

THEY CALL ME A REBEL
© 2005 Connor Tifarra, Connor Tifarra Entertainment

40 LONG DAYS

© 2015 Connor Tifarra, Connor Tifarra Entertainment

Drivin' down the road
Haulin' a load
Going wherever the load needs to go
Makin' good time
Jammin' through the state lines
In the sunshine, rain or snow
Counting down the days to go
Until I get back home

There are not many places that I haven't been
My truck has been on every road
Every scale I've been weighed in
I never had an overload

I love what I do
Though it's hard for me and you
Each day I'm one day closer to you
When I see our city lights coming into view
I'll know I'm almost home
From 40 long days on the road

It's been 40 long days and 40 long nights
Since I last kissed my baby goodbye
Travlin' down the road a hundred miles to go
I'll be home tonight
Lovin' my honey all night
When I get back home

Thousands of sunsets have shined in my eyes
And thousands of nights have filled the skies
I'm thinking about the love in your eyes
I'm going to see tonight

I love what I do
Though it's hard for me and you
Each day I'm one day closer to you
When I see our city lights coming into view
I'll know I'm almost home
From 40 long days on the road

It's been 40 long days and 40 long nights
Since I last kissed my baby goodbye
Travlin' down the road a hundred miles to go
I'll be home tonight
Lovin' my honey all night
When I get back home

The miles keep getting shorter
As I'm crossing every border
Truckin' across the USA
Solid white lines means I'm making good time
Jammin' gears all the way

Drivin' down the road
Haulin' a load
Going wherever the load needs to go
Makin' good time
Jammin' through the state lines
In the sunshine, rain or snow
Counting down to the days to go

Until I get back home

It's been 40 long days and 40 long nights
Since I last kissed my baby goodbye
Travlin' down the road a hundred miles to go
I'll be home tonight
Lovin' my honey all night
When I get back home
When I get back home
From 40 days on the road

40 LONG DAYS
© 2015 Connor Tifarra, Connor Tifarra Entertainment

IT'S BEEN A GOOD LIFE
© 2005 Connor Tifarra, Connor Tifarra Entertainment

I took a trip around the world
I met a beautiful girl
She stepped right out of my dreams
She is all I need

She said I love you
When we were sitting on her front porch swing
I reached into my pocket
And pulled out an engagement ring

Please be my wife
I said to her on one knee
I was shaking when she said yes
It was love in the first degree

We have traveled all around the world
We gave life to a boy and a girl
We watched them grow
We watched ourselves grow old
It's been a good life

I'm glad I took the time
To see the forest for the trees
To learn what's precious to me
You are all I need

Hey pretty lady

Come on and dance with me
Let's steal the night away
Under the stars just you and me

Times have changed and so have we
But nothing changed our love
We were right from the very start
It's you I've always dreamed of

We sit and talk of old times
We share our memories
Our youth comes back in our minds
We can make the clock unwind

Oh my sweet lady
Take my hand and follow me
Let's run like when we were young
Running wild and so carefree

I'm so happy
I see the forest for the trees
Our love will stand the test of time
Forever it's you and me

Put your loving arms around me
I'll hold you tenderly
Just like we were young
Sitting on your front porch swing

I know what love is
Love is loving you
That's all I ever wanted

It's been a good life loving you
It's been a good life
(It's been a good life)

It's been a good life
(Such a good life)

It's been a good life
(It's been a good life)

It's been a good life
(It's been such a good life)

It's been a good life
(It's been a good life)

It's been a good life
(It's been such a good life)
Loving you

IT'S BEEN A GOOD LIFE
© 2005 Connor Tifarra, Connor Tifarra Entertainment

I TRIPPED AND FELL IN LOVE

© 2010 Connor Tifarra, Connor Tifarra Entertainment

I was in the right place at just the right time
To see you walking by
When you least expect it to come your way
Loves finds its way to you

I don't know how I passed you by
I must have been looking at the sky
This fast paced world almost led me astray
Until I met you on the corner that day

The timing was right
To see each other in the sunlight
It was love at first sight
When I saw her eyes shine brightly
She smiled and said hello
Ever since that day I've loved her so

Love can sneak up on you
It's a crazy thing
Somehow love found you
And brought you all the way to me

I don't know how love does it
I only know I love it
I never thought I'd fall in love
But I tripped and fell in love that day

I use to fall too hard and love passed me up
This time I stumbled
But I had good luck
Now she loves me and my pick-up truck
I tripped and fell in love

mmm..., mmm, mmm, mmm, mmm
mmm, mmm, mmm, mmm, mmm
mmm..., mmm, mmm, mmm, mmm
mmm, mmm, mmm, mmm, mmm

The timing was right
To see each other in the sunlight
It was love at first sight
When I saw her eyes shine brightly
She smiled and said hello
Ever since that day I've loved her so

Love can sneak up on you
It's a crazy thing
Somehow love found you
And brought you all the way to me

I don't know how love does it
I only know I love it
I never thought I'd fall in love
But I tripped and fell in love that day

I use to fall too hard and love passed me up
This time I stumbled
But I had good luck
Now she loves me and my pick-up truck

I tripped and fell in love

mmm..., mmm, mmm, mmm, mmm
mmm, mmm, mmm, mmm, mmm
mmm..., mmm, mmm, mmm, mmm
mmm, mmm, mmm, mmm, mmm

I TRIPPED AND FELL IN LOVE
© 2010 Connor Tifarra, Connor Tifarra Entertainment

YESTERDAY WAS A DAMN GOOD DAY

© 2005 Connor Tifarra, Connor Tifarra Entertainment

I was enjoying my day just me and my wife
There was a knock on the door that changed my life

It was the county Sheriff and all his men
He said, "You're under arrest, I'm gonna run you in."
I said, "What's the charge? I didn't commit a crime!"
He said, "Shut your mouth boy. I know that you're lying.
I'm taking you in for killing your best friend.
You took your gun and done Big Jim in."

I was surprised and asked, "What happened to him?
He's my old friend, I wouldn't kill Big Jim."
Sheriff said, "You might look surprised but I can see right through your lies.
Big Jim was shot right between the eyes.
You know you shot him right between the eyes."

I had no choice I was caught in a trap
And I was wishing I could have yesterday back

Yesterday was a damn good day
What a damn good day it was
So much better than it is today
What a damn good day it was

I went into court

The trial was on
Twelve jurors stared at me, I knew I was done
Big Jim's kin said, "Yeah, he's the one that pulled the trigger of that .38 gun."

I took the witness stand to tell my side
I said, "I wasn't even there when Big Jim died."
I told the truth, I had nothing to hide
The jury said, "He's Guilty!"
All the witnesses lied

The Judge looked at me with his stone cold eyes
He said, "I sentence you to life!
Anything you'd like to say before I take you away?"
I said, "Yes Judge, this ain't right.
I've been wrongly accused of this terrible crime.
I didn't kill Big Jim he was a friend of mine."

He sent me off to prison to do my time
Forced behind bars and walking the line
And I remember what I thought that day
When the Sheriff came knocking and took me away

Yesterday was a damn good day
What a damn good day it was
Yesterday was a damn good day
What a damn good day it was

Now my hands are callused
My beards growing long
Shoveling coal I know I'll never see home
If only I had been with Big Jim that day

I wouldn't be here, he'd be alive today
I wouldn't be sitting in an 8 x 10 cell
The killer should be sitting here you know damn well

After years of rotting in this cold dark cell
I don't believe there's heaven, there's only hell
What do you expect from a convicted man?
Wrongfully sentenced for killing Big Jim
Sometimes it doesn't pay to be a man's friend
You might find yourself in prison until the very end

I remember what I was thinking that day
When the Sheriff came in and dragged me away
Yesterday was my last good day

Yesterday was a damn good day
What a damn good day it was
Yesterday was a damn good day
What a damn good day it was

YESTERDAY WAS A DAMN GOOD DAY
© 2005 Connor Tifarra, Connor Tifarra Entertainment

BROKEN PROMISES

© 2004 Connor Tifarra, Connor Tifarra Entertainment

You promised me a better life
You said everything would be alright
All we seem to do is fight
Nothing has worked out right
I can't go on living this way
I've got a future no matter what you say

I'm not going to fall with you to the ground
I'm going to stand tall no one can bring me down
You broke every promise
You broke my heart
Our love was a game
You won from the start

I always had faith that you'd change
Now I can see there's just no way
All my faith has gone away

All you ever gave me were broken promises
I thought you really loved me
How wrong I was
We wasted so much time
I thought I was yours
I thought you were mine
But I don't need your broken promises

Our world fell apart with all your secrecy

There's no way back to what we use to be
You broke every promise
You tore us apart
You killed every dream
You shot me in the dark

I know that you'll never change
You'll always be exactly the same
That's why I have to walk away

All you ever gave me were broken promises
I thought you really loved me
How wrong I was
We wasted so much time
I thought I was yours
I thought you were mine
But I don't need your broken promises

I'd never do what you did to me
I'd never make a promise that I couldn't keep
It seems you live a life full of lies
You hurt me so deep inside

What happened to you?
What made you this way?
Why did you tell me things you didn't mean to say?
Why did you lie?
What did you think you'd gain?
I dried my eyes
I broke free from your chains

It's you that needs to learn how to change

But we both know there's just no way
My life is starting over today

Because all you ever gave me were broken promises
I thought you really loved me
How wrong I was
We wasted so much time
I thought I was yours
I thought you were mine
But I don't need your broken promises
No more broken promises

BROKEN PROMISES
© 2004 Connor Tifarra, Connor Tifarra Entertainment

NOTHING LASTS

© 2004 Connor Tifarra, Connor Tifarra Entertainment

There's something about you that I can't explain
My hearts doing flips driving me insane
But the days go by
I'm wasting time
I want to make you mine

Soon you'll be in someone else's arms
Making love and giving all of your charm
It wouldn't have to be this way
If I only had the words to say

How will I ever know?
How will I ever see?
If I keep my dreams locked deep inside
My mind will never be free

Nothing seems to last forever
The sooner the better it's now or never
I don't know how long I'll wait
If I wait too long it may be too late

Every day I want to tell you I love you
But something inside me makes me scared as hell
I don't know when I'll get the courage
I guess only time will tell
But the days go by
I'm still wasting time

I should say what's on my mind

How will I ever know?
How will I ever see?
If I keep my dreams locked deep inside
My mind will never be free

Nothing seems to last forever
The sooner the better it's now or never
I don't know how long I'll wait
If I wait too long it may be too late

'Cause nothing seems to last forever
The sooner the better it's now or never
Nothing seems to last forever
The sooner the better it's now or never

NOTHING LASTS
© 2004 Connor Tifarra, Connor Tifarra Entertainment

LET'S FLY AWAY

© 2004 Connor Tifarra, Connor Tifarra Entertainment

There's never been a love like ours
On the planet Earth or the universe
I give you the heavens and the stars

You know I've never been to Mars
I've dreamed of traveling to the stars with you
Our love is true

Let's build a rocket and fly away
We'll live our life our own way
Don't be afraid
I'll show you the way

Let's fly away
Take my hand it will be ok
Let's fly away, fly away

Our love is new but meant to last
Forever we'll be, you don't have to ask
Eternity is on our side

We won't have to run and hide
Or keep our love locked deep inside
We'll be free, to do as we please

Let's build a rocket and fly away
We'll live our life our own way

Don't be afraid
I'll show you the way

Let's fly away
Take my hand it will be ok
Let's fly away, fly away

We'll always be together
It's you and me forever
Just like the world we were meant to be
We'll find a planet we can inhabit
Just you wait and see
Oh how I love you
Fly away with me

Let's fly away
Take my hand it will be ok
Let's fly away, fly away

TWO YOUNG LOVERS

© 2005 Connor Tifarra, Connor Tifarra Entertainment

We are two young lovers
Loving each other
We'll always be together
Just you and me
No matter what they say
No one can break us away
Today, tomorrow and forever

I give you my heart
It's yours to keep
I'll always be yours for all eternity
I'll cherish you for all my life
And always be by your side

I'll sit at the top of the world with you
No one can tell us what we should do
We'll hold on to each other
No one can break through
Because no one can stop two young lovers
From loving each other

The worries of life will all fade away
Time is on our side
Don't be afraid
We'll find the strength we need
Love will be our guide

I hear some people say we're just too young
They don't really know us
They are so wrong
No matter what they say
They can't take us away
Today, tomorrow and forever

I'll sit at the top of the world with you
No one can tell us what we should do
We'll hold on to each other
No one can break through
Because no one can stop two young lovers
From loving each other

I'll sit at the top of the world with you
No one can tell us what we should do
We'll hold on to each other
No one can break through
Because no one can stop two young lovers
From loving each other

TWO YOUNG LOVERS
© 2005 Connor Tifarra, Connor Tifarra Entertainment

NEXT TIME YOU'RE LONELY

© 2006 Connor Tifarra, Connor Tifarra Entertainment

Are you nervous?
Are you scared?
Did you think I wouldn't care?
I've been waiting right here for you all the while

In the daytime
In the night
I'll be there when things aren't right
I'll give comfort to you
I'll try to make you smile

I've had those feelings
The same as you
You're not alone
Sometimes I'm lonely like you

Next time you're lonely
I'll help you through your day
I'm only a phone call away
Next time you need me
I'll do anything for you
So you won't have to be so lonely

I would take you away to a secret place
I'd spend the day with you
And if by the night
There's still loneliness in sight

I'd stay right there with you
Because I'm lonely too

When you're feeling down and blue
Remember I might feel that way too
I know you'd do the same for me
As I would for you

Don't be nervous
Don't be scared
Now you know I've always cared
You don't have to be alone
I'll always be there

I comprehend what you've been through
You're not alone
Sometimes I'm lonely like you

Next time you're lonely
I'll help you through your day
I'm only a phone call away
Next time you need me
I'll do anything for you
So you won't have to be so lonely

Next time you're lonely
You don't have to hide
I'll be right by your side
Next time you need me
Don't you run away
You can always count on me
Next time you're lonely

Oh, oh next time
Next time you're lonely

NEXT TIME YOU'RE LONELY
© 2006 Connor Tifarra, Connor Tifarra Entertainment

WATCHING THE WAGON WHEEL ROLL 'ROUND

© 2003 Connor Tifarra, Connor Tifarra Entertainment

When I was only 10 years old my Papa came to me
He said, "Son, you need to pack your things, it's time to move our family.
We're going to California
We're going to find our destiny
So, you and Becky get in the wagon, wait for Ma and me."

I packed my bag
I climbed inside
Becky sat there scared
Then Mama climbed inside with a bible in her hand
It was time to leave
We went ridin' across the land
I remember,

Watching the wagon wheel roll 'round
Taking us to another town
Down the long and winding trail
Over the mountains, through the trees
Down through the valley streams
I wondered if I'd grow to be a man
Travlin' and livin' across the land

My little sister Becky, she died along the way
She caught the typhoid fever and God took her away
Papa led the way and Mama cried for days

And as we traveled on, I watched her tombstone fade away

We got to California after months of riding hard
Mama was so weary and Papa was so tired
We made our destination
Ma and Pa and me
And I knew my sister Becky was watching over me

Somehow through the years, I grew to be a man
Travlin' and livin' across this land
I remember,

Watching the wagon wheel roll 'round
Taking us to another town
Down the long and winding trail
Over the mountains, through the trees
Down through the valley streams
I wondered if I'd grow to be a man
Travlin' and livin' across the land

Now the years have passed, it seems I went from 10 to 93
I'm the last survivor to remember my family
And I'll always thank the Lord
For all he's done for me
And I know Ma and Pa and Becky
Are in heaven, waiting there for me

WATCHING THE WAGON WHEEL ROLL 'ROUND
© 2003 Connor Tifarra, Connor Tifarra Entertainment

THE BRAVE

© 2003 Connor Tifarra, Connor Tifarra Entertainment

I live and I breathe in the land of the brave
Proud of my country in so many ways
The air is so sweet
The grass is so green
The most beautiful place that I've ever seen

It's where dreams come true if you want them to
There's no end to what you can do
Oh how I love the USA

America, America
Land of hope and the free
America, America
God bless the home of the brave

This land is built on love, trust and faith
We open our arms to all religions and race
No turning our backs on people in need
We help everyone that wants to live free

We lend our hand to every country in the world
To keep freedom and peace for every boy and girl
Oh how I love the USA

America, America
Land of hope and the free
America, America

God bless the home of the brave

We dream of peace for the world
But we can't do it on our own
We need everyone to help us reach that goal
Remember our children they need us so

America
Home of the free
Where our forefathers fought for our liberty
They lived and died for you and me
God bless the home of the brave
God bless the home of the brave

THE BRAVE
© 2003 Connor Tifarra, Connor Tifarra Entertainment

RAINY DAY GIRL

© 2005 Connor Tifarra, Connor Tifarra Entertainment

You wandered around
When rainy days got you down
You thought the whole world was falling around you
I found you alone
No love of your own
No one to hold you when you're feeling lonely

I saw you so many times
When you'd walk by I knew I had to know you
Couldn't get you off my mind
That's when I knew that I just had to have you
To feel you
To make love to you

I could walk in the rain by your side
Then you wouldn't need the rain to hide the tears you cry
When rainy days get you down
I would always be around
Then you wouldn't be alone in this world
I'll be your rainy day girl

I didn't have the courage to say hello
The something deep inside me said don't let him go
This is my chance I better take it now
Or I'll never know just how I might have changed his world
I'll be his rainy day girl

Now you're my man
I'm your rainy day girl
Our two worlds collided with each other
Hand in hand in the sun
Two hearts became one
Loving each other
Best friends and best lovers

You're not alone
You have a love of your own
Someone to hold you when you're feeling lonely
I will always be near
No need to fear, I'll be with you forever
All your tears will disappear
And we'll be
Together
Forever

Now I walk in the rain by your side
And there are no more tears for the rain to hide
Sunny days are abound
True love's what we found
Love is all around us

I'm so glad
I'm your rainy day girl
True love's what we found
Love is all around us

It makes me happy
To be your rainy day girl
True love's what we found

Love is all around us
I'm so happy
To be your rainy day girl
True love's what we found
Love is all around us
There's someone for everyone
You'll be my only one
True love's what we found
Love is all around us

I'm so glad
I'm your rainy day girl
True love's what we found
Love is all around us

RAINY DAY GIRL
© 2005 Connor Tifarra, Connor Tifarra Entertainment

YOU'RE MY RAINY DAY GIRL
© 2005 Connor Tifarra, Connor Tifarra Entertainment

I use to wander around
When rainy days got me down
I thought the whole world was falling around me
You found me alone
No love of my own
No one to hold me when I felt so lonely

I saw you so many times
When I'd walk by I wished that I could know you
Couldn't get you off my mind
That's when I knew that I just had to have you
To feel you
To make love to you

Now we walk in the rain side by side
And I don't need the rain to hide the tears if I cry
When rainy days get me down
I know you'll always be around
I'll never be alone in this world
You're my rainy day girl

I didn't think I'd know you
Or even stand a chance
You told me that you loved me from the very first glance
I'm glad you had the courage to say hello
I'll never let you go
You came and changed my world

You're my rainy day girl

Now I'm your man
You're my rainy day girl
Our two worlds collided with each other
Hand in hand in the sun
Two hearts became one
Loving each other
Best friends and best lovers

I'm not alone
You're the love of my own
Always to hold me when I'm feeling lonely
I know you'll always be near
No need to fear, I'll be with you forever
All my tears have disappeared
And we'll be
Together
Forever

Now we walk in the rain side by side
There are no more tears
I don't have to hide
The sun is shining all around
True love's what we found
Love is all around us

I'm so glad
You're my rainy day girl
True love's what we found
Love is all around us

It makes me happy
You're my rainy day girl
True love's what we found
Love is all around us

I'm so happy
You're my rainy day girl
True love's what we found
Love is all around us

There's someone for everyone
You'll be my only one
True love's what we found
Love is all around us

I'm so glad
You're my rainy day girl
True love's what we found
Love is all around us

YOU'RE MY RAINY DAY GIRL
© 2005 Connor Tifarra, Connor Tifarra Entertainment

21 LOVERS LANE

© 2006 Connor Tifarra, Connor Tifarra Entertainment

I wish that Cancer was just an astrological sign
The disease that shares the same name
Took the girl that was mine

She was young
And full of fun
Her life had just begun

She had a smile that was bright
Eyes that shined in the night
She liked everyone

She had a heart full of love
She loved God above
I loved her and she loved me

Her favorite place
Was Sunset Beach
At 21 Lovers Lane

We use to walk all the way
To 21 Lovers Lane
Watching the ocean
Drinking champagne
Dancing to the band
Walk the beach hand in hand
Watching the sun fade away

Just me and my girl
In our corner of the world
At 21 Lovers Lane

That's the way that it was
We shared each other's love
It seems like yesterday

I miss the look in your eyes
Staring at the skies
Wondering what tomorrow would bring

But one day
Tomorrow never came
Time stopped at 21 Lovers Lane

The Sun forgot to rise
Clouds filled the skies
Down came the rain

Smiles turned to tears
Happy memories erased the fears
That day I lost a friend
I thought of where it all began
On Sunset Beach

We use to walk all the way
To 21 Lovers Lane
Watching the ocean
Drinking champagne
Dancing to the band
Walk the beach hand in hand

Watching the sun fade away

Just me and my girl
In our corner of the world
At 21 Lovers Lane
21 Lovers Lane
21 Lovers Lane

LETTING GO OF LOVE

© 2009 Connor Tifarra, Connor Tifarra Entertainment

I heard you found someone new
That you can tell all of your lies to
I feel bad for him
He's in the same situation you put me in

What will it take?
For you to see the mistakes you've been making?
If you're doing to him what you did to me
I know his heart is breaking

Because you were easy to love
'Till I knew what you were made of
There's no easy way
No good words to say
When love starts slipping away

Losing a friend
Starting over again
Sometimes we learn the hard way
It's fun to fall in love
But letting go of love isn't easy

It's hard on your mind
It's hard on your heart
When the one you love says they want to part
We live and we learn
Sometimes love can't return

And we both have to go our own way
It feels so good to fall in love
But letting go of love isn't easy

You helped me to see
What I needed for me
No more hanging on
I was hanging too long
Our dreams started fading away

Time passed us by
We didn't see eye to eye
But we both saw our love drift away

There was no going back
To what we use to have
The past was done and so were we
It was fun to fall in love
But letting go of love isn't easy

It's hard on your mind
It's hard on your heart
When the one you love says they want to part
We live and we learn
Sometimes love can't return
And we both have to go our own way
It feels so good to fall in love
But letting go of love isn't easy
Letting go of love isn't easy

LETTING GO OF LOVE
© 2009 Connor Tifarra, Connor Tifarra Entertainment

ROSES, RAINBOWS AND YOU

© 2007 Connor Tifarra, Connor Tifarra Entertainment

Long ago we planted a garden full of roses
Each one brings back memories of you
Today I saw a rainbow above our garden
And I chased it the way we used to do

I felt just like I did back then
You and me running in the wind
Never reaching the rainbows end
All the gold we needed was in our love

We loved blue skies
We loved the rain
We watched our roses through the windowpane
The garden still looks the same
The only thing missing is you

I love to watch the roses grow
Waiting for the next rainbow
Try to catch it before it goes away

Touch the colors
Smell the air
The scent from roses fills the air
Pretty colors everywhere
All that's missing is you

We planted white roses along the pathway

It almost felt like walking through a cloud
You looked like an angel in our garden
With beautiful roses all around

I'd watch you sit on your favorite bench
Think in the rain until your dress was drenched
The only thing between you and the sun
Were the clouds and the raindrops

We loved blue skies
We loved the rain
We watched our roses through the windowpane
The garden still looks the same
The only thing missing is you

I love to watch the roses grow
Waiting for the next rainbow
Try to catch it before it goes away

Touch the colors
Smell the air
The scent from roses fills the air
Pretty colors everywhere
All that's missing is you

Each year I watch our roses grow
And I learned long ago
There are three things that I love so
Our roses, rainbows and you

ROSES, RAINBOWS AND YOU
© 2007 Connor Tifarra, Connor Tifarra Entertainment

LOOKING AT THE OUTSIDE

© 2011 Connor Tifarra, Connor Tifarra Entertainment

You're always looking at the outside
Never looking at the inside
How will you ever know if you're really in love?

If someone's going to love you and show that they care
Don't you run away
Don't you be scared
Give them a chance to say how they really feel

You never let your love light show
You're all alone again
You're afraid they'll always let you go
You're on your own again
You never look within

You haven't learned your lesson yet
What you see isn't always what you get
You can't judge just by the cover
That's not the way to love her
You've got to see under the skin

Stop looking on the outside
Try looking at the inside
That's when you'll really know
You found your true love

You have to take the time to learn who she is

Don't just be her lover
Be her best friend
Put on the breaks and do whatever it takes

Show her that she's more than a passing fling
A girl you can love
Make her heart sing
Let her know you mean what you really feel

You never let your love light show
You're all alone again
You're afraid they'll always let you go
You're on your own again
You never look within

You haven't learned your lesson yet
What you see isn't always what you get
You can't judge just by the cover
That's not the way to love her
You've got to see under the skin

Stop looking on the outside
Try looking at the inside
That's when you'll really know
You found your true love

Stop looking at the outside
Try looking at the inside
That's when you will know you're really in love

LOOKING AT THE OUTSIDE
© 2011 Connor Tifarra, Connor Tifarra Entertainment

HOLLY

© 2005 Connor Tifarra, Connor Tifarra Entertainment

Let me paint a picture for you
Of the prettiest girl I ever knew
She had bright blue eyes and long blonde hair
She looked like a dream I dreamed somewhere
I look for you but you're nowhere

Holly won't you come back home
Please don't leave me all alone
Holly won't you come back home
I don't want to dream alone
Holly, please come home

I woke one day and you weren't there
Just your make-up on the dresser
And an empty chair
No reflection in the mirror
Nights are lonely without you near
I wish you were here

Holly won't you come back home
Please don't leave me all alone
Holly won't you come back home
I don't want to dream alone
Holly, please come home

Love can sometimes make us blind
Two hearts that once shined

Are now lost in time
Somehow we'll both find our way
Won't you come back to me and stay

Holly won't you come back home
Please don't leave me all alone
Holly won't you come back home
Don't leave me dreaming all alone

Holly won't you come back home
Please don't leave me all alone
Holly won't you come back home
Don't leave me dreaming all alone
Holly, please come
Holly, please come home

HOLLY
© 2005 Connor Tifarra, Connor Tifarra Entertainment

TIME PLAYS THE GAME
© 2003 Connor Tifarra, Connor Tifarra Entertainment

Time plays the game
Until it's over
Watching it slip away
Until it's gone

If I had my way
I'd change it to be any time I wanted
Time and time again
How I've wondered

Time plays the game
Time plays the game

Time has always had its way
With comedy and tragedy
Taking things away from me
A memory lost in time

New life replaces all the death
Time erases all regrets
Time brings the sunshine
And time brings the rain

The people cannot see it
But deep inside they feel it
Time runs in your heart
And it travels through your veins

Time plays the game
Time plays the game

Reflections change throughout the years
Broken dreams and shattered mirrors
Pieces of your life appear
Scattered across the floor

The past cannot be found again
It lives in memories deep within
Time eats the days away
And it swallows all the nights

While searching for your peace of mind
You know your time will come to die
Time leaves it all behind
It will close and lock the door

Time plays the game
Time plays the game

Standing at the wishing well
I heard the sacred tower bells
Ringing through the valley
Echoing across the plains

One life is all you get to live
Time has no beginning and it has no end
It will always see the sunshine
And it will always bring the rain

History has proven

Through the relics and the ruins
Nothing lasts forever
Its only time that wins the game

Time plays the game
Time plays the game

Time plays the game
Wishful thoughts that I have pondered
Time and time again
How I've wondered

If I had my way
I'd change it to be any time I wanted
It would not be the same without you

TIME PLAYS THE GAME
© 2003 Connor Tifarra, Connor Tifarra Entertainment

TRAPPED

© 2004 Connor Tifarra, Connor Tifarra Entertainment

You've got me suffocated
No room to breathe I really hate it
I'm sick of being trapped
I'm taking my life back
For me

Did you think about me?
Or was it only of yourself?
You tried to shut me out
You never gave a damn
About me

You finally got me thinkin'
Its freedom I've been seekin'
It doesn't matter what you say
Nothing can make me stay

I feel trapped
I'm gonna fight back
Got to get out
No one can hold me back
I feel trapped
I've got to escape
I'm movin' on
I'm gettin' out of this place
I'm taking off my mask
I'm taking my life back

I don't want to be trapped

Feel like I'm on an island
I'm all alone and isolated
Watching ships go by
Leaving me to die
Alone

My head is such a mess
I'm tearing down this fence
You can't stop me

'Cuz you finally got me thinkin'
Its freedom I've been seekin'
It doesn't matter what you say
Nothing can make me stay

I feel trapped
I'm gonna fight back
Got to get out
No one can hold me back
I feel trapped
I've got to escape
I'm movin' on
I'm gettin' out of this place
I'm taking off my mask
I'm taking my life back
I don't want to be trapped

No more suffocation
No more strangulation
I'm breaking free today

Get out of my way
You can't stop me

'Cuz you finally got me thinkin'
Its freedom I've been seekin'
It doesn't matter what you say
Nothing can make me stay

I feel trapped
I'm gonna fight back
Got to get out
No one can hold me back
I feel trapped
I've got to escape
I'm movin' on
I'm gettin' out of this place
I'm taking off my mask
I'm taking my life back
I don't want to be trapped

TURN MY LIFE AROUND
© 2004 Connor Tifarra, Connor Tifarra Entertainment

Why do you push me around?
You call me names and you knock me down
I was such a fool for loving you
I did the best that I could do
What about you?

You think that you can control me
Let me tell you baby you're so wrong
I'll live life the way I want to
It's too late to work things through
I'm not gonna be like you

'Cuz I live for life, love and freedom
I need something good to believe in
I know I'll find someone
That loves me for everything I've done
I'm not gonna let you bring me down
I'll turn my life around

Don't you think you could have tried a little harder?
You shoved me off the edge
Drowned me in deep water
But I'm still alive
I know how to survive

It's a shame I have to go
It hurts me more than you could know

I know as time goes by
I won't even think to cry
I'll do the best that I can do
What about you?

I live for life, love and freedom
I need something good to believe in
I know I'll find someone
That loves me for everything I've done
I'm not gonna let you bring me down
I'll turn my life around

I live for life, love and freedom
I need something good to believe in
I know I'll find someone
That loves me for everything I've done
I'm not gonna let you bring me down
I'll turn my life around
I'll turn my life around
I'll turn my life around

TURN MY LIFE AROUND
© 2004 Connor Tifarra, Connor Tifarra Entertainment

DELUSIONS

© 2005 Connor Tifarra, Connor Tifarra Entertainment

It's a crying shame
You never did the things you said
You lost everything
You had delusions in your head
Look where it's got you now
You never opened up
You live inside yourself
You're paying the price right now
You're going to self destruct
You know damn well

Too bad you got lost
You didn't think about the cost
Never heard a word I said
Forgot your family and your friends
You always thought no one could tell
But you were only fooling, fooling yourself
What do you expect from me?
You're out of touch with reality

Your mind is filled with mass confusion
You wake up in the night to your inner illusions
Lost in seclusion, trapped inside your head

You never believed me
You have no trust
Your paranoid delusions have ruined us

You always turn your back when times get tough
You're only fooling yourself
You're out of touch

You'll end up alone
Walking the streets nowhere to go
Shaking from the cold
No one to love you anymore
How could you want to be that way?
I guess you made your choice
I tried to help you change
You never gave a damn what I had to say

You never believed me
You have no trust
Your paranoid delusions have ruined us
You always turn your back when times get tough
You're only fooling yourself
You're out of touch

Your mind is filled with mass confusion
You wake up in the night to your inner illusions
Lost in seclusion, trapped inside your head

You never stop to smell the roses
All you think about are false delusions
Wake up and get those thoughts out of your head
You're only fooling yourself
You're out of touch

DELUSIONS
© 2005 Connor Tifarra, Connor Tifarra Entertainment

I'M FEELING DOWN

© 2004 Connor Tifarra, Connor Tifarra Entertainment

I thought I'd try to write a song
'Bout how we laughed all night long
And the times I thought you loved me

I lay down and cry alone at night
I wonder if you'll see the light
Life is so lonely without you

There are no words that can express
How my heart is left with emptiness
You promised me we'd never part
So if you ever change your mind
I'll be here for you to find
Please take a chance and turn around
I'm feeling down

I see your reflection in the mirror
A part of you, lives with me here
Broken glass and shattered dreams
Cut me up and torture me

We used to love each other
Where did we go wrong?
You were always putting me down
Your words cut me to the bone
I'd rather be alone

I light a smoke and hang my head
I wonder if I'll see you again
Dreams of you are all I see
Let me end this misery

The only words that I can say
To tell you how I feel today
You broke your promise, you broke my heart
But if you ever change your mind
I'll be here for you to find
Please take a chance and turn around
I'm feeling down
I'm feeling down
Ohh, ohh I'm down
Ohh, ohh, ohh, ohh

I'M FEELING DOWN
© 2004 Connor Tifarra, Connor Tifarra Entertainment

I'LL HAVE TO DREAM ALONE
© 2004 Connor Tifarra, Connor Tifarra Entertainment

It suddenly came to my mind
That the rivers washed away the time
I'm not getting any younger
But how I hunger

Sunshine escapes from my heart
Like the tides of the ocean we drift apart
Our love can be saved
Maybe I'll catch a wave

I cry in the rain to hide my pain
Teardrops fall driving me insane
How can I ever explain?

Dreams of you seem to fade and go
As time goes by how will I ever know?
All I wanted was for you to be my own
But for now I'll have to dream alone

We laughed together
We walked hand in hand
Our smiles turned to tears
I didn't understand
We changed in different ways
We let love slip away

You turned your back to me and walked away

I watched you go I didn't want it this way
What could I say?
To make you want to stay

I count the days that you've been away
I wonder how long I'll have to feel this pain
How can I ever explain?

Dreams of you seem to fade and go
As time goes by how will I ever know?
All I wanted was for you to be my own
But for now I'll have to dream alone

Won't you tell me I'm wrong and you're coming home?
I don't want to spend my whole life alone
Help me from drowning in the rain

I wish I could go back to a place in time
When nothing mattered but you and I
We were perfect lovers
We had each other

No matter where we go from here
I'll always remember you my dear
I'm not getting any younger
But how I hunger

Won't you tell me I'm wrong and you're coming home?
I don't want to spend my whole life alone
Help me from drowning in the rain

Dreams of you seem to fade and go

As time goes by how will I ever know?
All I wanted was for you to be my own
But for now I'll have to dream alone

I'LL HAVE TO DREAM ALONE
© 2004 Connor Tifarra, Connor Tifarra Entertainment

THE DECISION

© 2005 Connor Tifarra, Connor Tifarra Entertainment

I see you've made up your mind
You left it all behind
You threw me away
But that's ok
I'm sure we'll both get by
I guess I was blind
I didn't see your pain
Behind your eyes you live in the pouring rain

You kept your feelings inside
You didn't have to run and hide
That's a hard way to live
I was always here
But you never tried

I don't understand
Why you left when I was sleeping
I couldn't tell
'Cuz you hid all your feelings

Don't you think you made the wrong decision?
You never realized
You get what you're giving
The whole world's not to blame
When you lost everything
You're the only one to blame

Every day I wake up alone
It's no longer a happy home
So much has changed
It's just not the same without you

So many times we tried
Too many times you lied
But you didn't see
What that did to me
You hid your eyes

I know this time
I won't see you anymore
I hope you find
What it is you're looking for

Don't you think you made the wrong decision?
You never realized
You get what you're giving
The whole world's not to blame
When you lost everything
You're the only one to blame
It was your decision

Life can seem so hard
I know because I've been there
You read me wrong
Because I'm the one that really cared

I wish you had said goodbye
I wish you had took the time
That was so cold

Now you'll never know
That I never lied

I must have been blind
'Cuz I never saw it comin'
You lost all your pride
I thought that we had somethin'

Don't you think you made the wrong decision?
You never realized
You get what you're giving
The whole world's not to blame
When you lost everything
You're the only one
You're the only one
You're the only one to blame

THE DECISION
© 2005 Connor Tifarra, Connor Tifarra Entertainment

EXIT 41

© 2015 Connor Tifarra, Connor Tifarra Entertainment

Driving down the highway with my radio on
Next stop Exit 41
Headed to the pool room
Going to party on
I'm going to run the table all night long

Billiards is my game
I don't know her name
I like her ass and her skin tight pants
I like the way she bends

I like her style and the way she plays
She's burning hot in the first degree
She knows she distracts she gives me shaky knees
She's got notches on her stick from every man that she's beat

She came to get it on at Exit 41
9 balls on the table she'll run them all night long
She'll take all your money
She's a pool hall hustlin' honey
At Exit 41
Exit 41
Exit 41

She played her game just as smooth as can be
She stretched across the table she was such a tease
She knew how to distract a man and win the game

She drove the men insane

She made lots of money being a pool hall hustlin' honey
She made lots of green
She had her named engraved on her stick
She was 8-Ball Irene

She came to get it on at Exit 41
9 balls on the table she'll run them all night long
She'll take all your money
She's a pool hall hustlin' honey
At Exit 41
Exit 41
Exit 41

She racked the balls for one more game
She took me for everything
I lost all my money and my gold tooth too
She said, "It was a pleasure beating you"

Minnesota Fats wouldn't have stood a chance
Pretty Boy Floyd would have loved her pants
Willie Masconi would have took the fall
She knew every trick and she used them all

She came to get it on at Exit 41
9 balls on the table she'll run them all night long
She'll take all your money
She's a pool hall hustlin' honey
At Exit 41

Exit 41

(Better hope she's not there)
Exit 41
(She's a millionaire)
Exit 41
(You betcha')
Exit 41
(She's gonna getcha')
Exit 41
(Watch out)
Exit 41
Exit 41

EXIT 41
© 2015 Connor Tifarra, Connor Tifarra Entertainment

INVISIBLE

© 2015 Connor Tifarra, Connor Tifarra Entertainment

My dreams are transparent just like you and me
I'm invisible
You have eyes but you cannot see
I'm invisible

You built a wall made of dust, dirt and sand
You dwell within the barren land
How long will you hide in your dungeon of doom?
Blood falls through the hourglass
The end is coming soon

Moisture escapes from your mouth
You wish for rain but you've got to stick it out
What you see is what you get
All you see is nothing so nothings what you get

I'm invisible
I'm invisible
I'm invisible
You have eyes but you can't see me

You looked away and got burned by the flame
You're invisible
Russian roulette is your favorite game
You can't lose
You're invisible

No good words ever exit your mouth
Every time you speak only screams come out
What you see is what you get
All you see is nothing so nothings what you get

I'm invisible
I'm invisible
I'm invisible
You have eyes but you can't see me

Your dreams are transparent like you made mine be
You're invisible
You can't see what you've done to me
I'm invisible

That's not the cops banging on your door
That the guy upstairs stomping on the floor
That's not your reflection in the mirror
You're transparent
You're not even here

You're invisible
You're invisible
You're invisible
I look for you but I can't see

We're invisible
We're both invisible
We're invisible
We have eyes but cannot see

Everything's invisible

It's all invisible

I'm invisible
You're invisible

EXPENSIVE BITCH

© 2012 Connor Tifarra, Connor Tifarra Entertainment

She wants all your money
She wants everything
She wants a big fur coat
A green Ferrari
And a 10 carat diamond ring
Cash is her best friend
That's why she only dates the rich
She'll suck you dry
She won't say goodbye
She's a ruthless, heartless bitch

She wants your fortune
So you better give it all
Give her the cash
Or she'll be gone in a flash
Be at her beck and call
She'll get on her knees
If you give her what she needs
She'll spend it all
When it's all gone
She'll pack up and leave

She's an expensive bitch
It takes hundred dollar bills to scratch her itch
She's an expensive bitch
There's no doubt about it
She's an expensive bitch

She'll leave you broke in a ditch
She's an expensive bitch
She can't live without it

She wants to live in a mansion
She wants fancy cuisine
She wants caviar
Your credit cards
She thinks she's a Queen
You're not her boyfriend
You're an ATM machine
She'll get you up
She'll knock you down
Man, this girl is mean

She's an expensive bitch
It takes hundred dollar bills to scratch her itch
She's an expensive bitch
There's no doubt about it
She's an expensive bitch
She'll leave you broke in a ditch
She's an expensive bitch
She can't live without it

She never loved you
She's only full of greed
She wants her name on a star
You won't go far
If you don't give her what she needs
It's money that matters
She only loves the color green
She'll bite like a shark

Rip out your heart
She'll take you for everything

She's an expensive bitch
It takes hundred dollar bills to scratch her itch
She's an expensive bitch
There's no doubt about it
She's an expensive bitch
She'll leave you broke in a ditch
She's an expensive bitch
She can't live without it

She's an expensive bitch
She only loves the color green
She's an expensive bitch
She's so mean
She's an expensive bitch
She's an expensive bitch

EXPENSIVE BITCH
© 2012 Connor Tifarra, Connor Tifarra Entertainment

ALL MY LIFE
© 2005 Connor Tifarra, Connor Tifarra Entertainment

All my life
I've been beaten when competin'
All my life
I always lose its so frustratin'

I know I'm gonna win
One way or another
I'm sick and tired of losing
When's it gonna be my turn

You know I keep on pushin'
I'm never gonna stop
I'm never givin' up
I'm gonna be on top because

All my life
I've been beaten when competin'
All my life
I always lose its so frustratin'
All my life
I wanna win I'm tired of losin'
All my life
All this losin's so confusin'

I've takin' quite a beaten
People said, I think your cheatin'
You know I never did

I don't need to cheat to win

You know I keep on pushin'
I'm never gonna stop
I'm never givin' up
I'm gonna be on top because

All my life
I've been beaten when competin'
All my life
I always lose its so frustratin'
All my life
I wanna win I'm tired of losin'
All my life
All this losin's so confusin'

Nobody wants to be a loser
Will winning days ever come my way?
I've got to find a way
To be a winner for just one day

I'm tired of always being the loser
It seems I lose at everything
I've always lived a life of strife
Now it's time I win because

All my life
I've been beaten when competin'
All my life
I always lose its so frustratin'
All my life
I wanna win I'm tired of losin'

All my life
All this losin's so confusin'

All my life
I'm gonna be a winner
All my life
A winner not a quitter
All my life
I'm gonna keep on pushin'
All my life
Winning never losin'

HEART OF FIRE

© 2013 Connor Tifarra, Connor Tifarra Entertainment

In his heart burns an eternal flame
He carries with him the flame of pain
He'll strip the skin right off of your bones
His hearts on fire better leave him alone

He's played every game and he wins every time
He's the world's best pantomime
He won't tell you what you should do
He'll stand by just watching you

He's got a heart of fire
An eternal flame
Your dirty deeds are his claim to fame
Feeding his desire
Flames are reaching higher
Heart of fire

All the wars and killing is one hell of a game
Every time you take a life you feed the burning flame
The General pats your back and says, "Job well done!"
Pins a medal on chest and says, "Go do it again."

You listen to the man with your programmed brain
You're a killer not a lover what a crying shame
He loves what you're doing and you do it good
You don't pretend, this isn't Hollywood

He's got a heart of fire
An eternal flame
Your dirty deeds are his claim to fame
Feeding his desire
Flames are reaching higher
Heart of fire

You can run through the forest
You can run through the alley
There's nowhere to hide
From the watchful eye

Better bow your head
Get down on your knees
You better feed the fire
Higher and higher
Higher and higher
Higher and higher

He's got a heart of fire
An eternal flame
Your dirty deeds are his claim to fame
Feeding his desire
Flames are reaching higher
Heart of fire

He's got a heart of fire
Yeah his hearts on fire
Heart of fire
Heart of fire

HEART OF FIRE
© 2013 Connor Tifarra, Connor Tifarra Entertainment

TIC-TAC-DIE

© 2011 Connor Tifarra, Connor Tifarra Entertainment

I've made my move
Now you make yours
Make your choice wisely
There won't be any encores

It's a game of win or lose
There's no such thing as a tie
X marks the spot in war
The name of the game is TIC–TAC–DIE

From the earth's ground and seas
From the air and space
Weapons of mass destruction
Will murder the human race

Thinking they have something to prove
Each leader will make the wrong move
They'll send rockets soaring through the sky
Killing you and I
Knowing they can't win
They never give in
War is a game of TIC-TAC-DIE

The grid is marked with X's
Targets marked to strike
Silent drones drop the bombs
Killing in the night

They blow apart the buildings
They blow away bodies and brains
They kill women and children
Justifying it with God's name

The leaders never attack each other
They only kill the innocent lives
Gutless rulers of nations
Playing the game of TIC-TAC-DIE

Thinking they have something to prove
Each leader will make the wrong move
They'll send rockets soaring through the sky
Killing you and I
Knowing they can't win
They never give in
War is a game of TIC-TAC-DIE

The soldiers are pawns
Expendable dogs
Volunteering to die for a man in a suit
An eye for an eye is far from the truth

Brainwashed to obey their master's commands
The soldiers kill with unclean hands
They engrave their weapons with scriptures from the Holy Bible
Shooting projectiles of God into all the people

The politicians hide behind the desk
Making decisions with the stroke of a pen
Playing the game that no one can win

The game is TIC-TAC-DIE

Thinking they have something to prove
Each leader will make the wrong move
They'll send rockets soaring through the sky
Killing you and I
Knowing they can't win
They never give in
War is a game of TIC-TAC-DIE

It's a game of win or lose
There's no such thing as a tie
X marks the spot in war
The name of the game is TIC-TAC-DIE

TIC-TAC-DIE
© 2011 Connor Tifarra, Connor Tifarra Entertainment

UNDERCOVER LIES

© 2009 Connor Tifarra, Connor Tifarra Entertainment

Mafia boys
Government spies
Intelligent operations
Undercover lies

Creators of deception
Victims of their own game
Blinded by obsession
Don't trust a man with a plane

Pay-offs and wires
Eyes in the sky
Watching from all angles
Black wings on high

Manipulation
Sleight of hand
Mirror's of deception
The new promise land
Internal corruption
Deceit and spite
Slander and mayhem
Undercover lies

Living life on a leash
Hide behind doors
Conceal possessions

Peek through cracks in the floors

Outside smiles
Inner demise
Outer falsehoods
Inner disguise

Legions of the realm
False prophets on high
Promises to the people
Undercover lies

Manipulation
Sleight of hand
Mirror's of deception
The new promise land
Internal corruption
Deceit and spite
Slander and mayhem
Undercover lies

Undercover spies
You never see them coming
Because they're already there
Undercover lies
Right before your eyes
Jed he's a millionaire

Stirring the pot
Causing the fright
Secret observations
Undercover lies

Put out the candle
Dowse out the flame
Hope the boss doesn't know your name
He's out to get you
Better take a stand
Look out
For the undercover man

Manipulation
Sleight of hand
Mirror's of deception
The new promise land
Internal corruption
Deceit and spite
Slander and mayhem
Undercover lies

We live
With undercover lies

Like a fugitive
Undercover lies

Lucrative
Undercover lies

Definitive
Undercover lies

Undercover lies
Undercover lies
Undercover lies

Undercover lies
Undercover lies

UNDERCOVER LIES
© 2009 Connor Tifarra, Connor Tifarra Entertainment

THE AMERICAN DREAM

© 2010 Connor Tifarra, Connor Tifarra Entertainment

I'm an American
Living the American dream
Taking everything I can
Taking it all for me

I'll do what it takes
To fill my need for greed
I'll lie, cheat and steal
I'll even make you bleed

Don't turn your back
If you know I'm around
If you've got what I want
I'm going to cut you down

Let's fight
Let's have a war
I have all I could need
But I still want more
Let's fight
I want what you've got
I'm going to take it all
If you like it or not
I'm going to take it all
Whether you like it or not

I want your oil

I want your land
Give it before I take it
Understand?
I want your house
I want your car
I'll take your cookies
And the cookie jar

I'll do whatever
I think I need to do
Watch out
American coming through

Let's fight
Let's have a war
I have all I could need
But I still want more
Let's fight
I want what you've got
I'm going to take it all
If you like it or not
I'm going to take it all
Whether you like it or not

I want all your money
Give it to me now
Surrender your belongings
I'll send missiles off the bow

I'll plan and I'll scheme
That's the American dream
The land of take it for free

The land of do what I please

See what I mean?
That's the American dream
The American extreme
American supreme

Don't need a Constitution
Overrule any laws
Make yourself a world leader
Kill them all

Let's fight
Let's have a war
I have all I could need
But I still want more
Let's fight
I want what you've got
I'm going to take it all
If you like it or not
I'm going to take it all
Whether you like it or not

So let's fight
Let's have a war
I have all I could need
But I still want more
Let's fight
I want what you've got
I'm going to take it all
If you like it or not

I'm going to take it all
Take it all

THE AMERICAN DREAM
© 2010 Connor Tifarra, Connor Tifarra Entertainment

DEFENESTRATION

© 2011 Connor Tifarra, Connor Tifarra Entertainment

How high can you jump?
How far will you fall?
How hard will you go splat?
From twenty stories tall

How long will you stand there?
Balancing on that ledge
Jump out far enough
Or you'll survive in the hedge

There's nothing left to live for
Only reasons to die
Climb high as you can
Fall from a clear blue sky

You're a wingless bird
You're a diving plane
You're a human projectile
Your blood drops of rain

Defenestration
A jumping celebration
Nosedive through the air
Like a shooting flare
Diving straight into hell
On a one-way ride
Soar like an eagle

Watch him fly

Sympathy can't be given
For the weakness of your soul
You chose to jump into the fire
You drilled your own hole

Taking a leap of faith
Testing chance and time
Eight seconds to freedom
No more crying

You soar through the wind
You swiftly fall to the ground
One minute you're still living
Next minute underground

Ending the pain
Ending the strife
A quitter with no glory
Such a wasted life

Defenestration
A jumping celebration
Nosedive through the air
Like a shooting flare
Diving straight into hell
On a one-way ride
Soar like an eagle
Watch him fly

You made the world stop turning

Though it was only for you
The living, keep on living
Your days are through

You left your peace of mind
In fragments on the ground
People stand there staring
No one makes a sound

There are no words to speak
Thoughts that can't be expressed
Staring at your lifeless body
Leaving hearts at unrest

The show is over
You went out with a bang
You bowed at the final curtain
You earned your fame

Now your eyes are closed
You'll never see again
You have become the darkness
You're dead but didn't win

Defenestration
A jumping celebration
Nosedive through the air
Like a shooting flare
Diving straight into hell
On a one-way ride
Soar like an eagle
Watch him fly

Defenestration
A jumping celebration
Nosedive through the air
Like a shooting flare
Diving straight into hell
On a one-way ride
Soar like an eagle
Watch him fly

Defenestration
A jumping celebration
Defenestration
Watch him fly

DEFENESTRATION
© 2011 Connor Tifarra, Connor Tifarra Entertainment

COUNTDOWN CLOCK

© 2010 Connor Tifarra, Connor Tifarra Entertainment

Time never stops
Time can't be reversed
The circle of life
Spins around the earth

You carry on your shoulders
And upon your back
The weight of the world
And burdens of the past

You're on the countdown to freedom
It started when you began
You're on the countdown to freedom
Time for your clock to stop
And let another begin

You take three steps forward
You check the time
Steadfast and ready
Not afraid to die

Your countdown clock
Ticks away in your heart
Tick-tock, Tick-tock
You're falling apart

You're on the countdown to freedom

It started when you began
You're on the countdown to freedom
Time for your clock to stop
And let another begin

Are you prepared to pay the price?
To make the ultimate sacrifice?
The cost of freedom will blow your mind
And send you soaring sky high

Let the darkness go
Let it stay in the past
Remember these words
Good things never last

Your countdown clock
Ticks away in your brain
Tick-tock, Tick-tock
Waiting for the sleep train

You're on the countdown to freedom
It started when you began
You're on the countdown to freedom
Time for your clock to stop
And let another begin

You're on the countdown to freedom
Countdown to freedom

You're on the countdown to freedom
Countdown to freedom

Tick-tock, Tick-tock
Time for your clock to stop

COUNTDOWN CLOCK
© 2010 Connor Tifarra, Connor Tifarra Entertainment

BETTER GO GET HER
© 2013 Connor Tifarra, Connor Tifarra Entertainment

You pissed her off
You screwed up again
You went to places
Where you shouldn't have been

There's no excuse
For being a jerk
You know what you did
You made your girl hurt

Better go get her
She's running away
You don't find a girl like that everyday
The girl is a keeper
Don't be a deceiver
Don't make her want to leave ya

Time to stand up
Be a man
Tell her you're sorry
You won't do it again

Don't just say it
Do what you say
Stop your bullshit
Then maybe she'll stay

Better go get her
She's running away
You don't find a girl like that everyday
The girl is a keeper
Don't be a deceiver
Don't make her want to leave ya

It's time you get a grip on reality
Grow up and be a man or set the woman free
Love's not a game and you know she isn't playing
Better go get her because she's up and leaving

There's a lesson to learn
If she doesn't return
Stop telling lies
Be home with her at night

Stop screwing around
All over town
Put down the booze
If you don't want to lose

Better go get her
She's running away
You don't find a girl like that everyday
The girl is a keeper
Don't be a deceiver
Don't make her want to leave ya

You better go get her
Don't be a fool
Better go get her

Or she'll leave you
Better go get her
Owww
Better go get her
Go get her right now
Better go get her
Better go get her
Better go get her
You better go get her

BETTER GO GET HER
© 2013 Connor Tifarra, Connor Tifarra Entertainment

I'M COMING HOME FOR CHRISTMAS

© 2004 Connor Tifarra, Connor Tifarra Entertainment

I'm leaving for Memphis on a railway train
I can't wait to be home for the holidays
Many years I've been gone
Lord it's been too long
But I'm coming home for Christmas

Time just seems to go on by so fast
The years they just pass
And each year I missed you more
There's so much I have to say
I've waited for this day
We'll finally be together at last

So, don't you cry
Wipe the tears from your eyes

This year, you won't have to be so lonely
Don't fear, I'll be there so you can hold me
I've waited for this day to be here
I'm coming home for Christmas this year

Looking out the window of the train
We roll through the plains
And I sit here thinking of you
All my memories fill my mind
I know this time we'll never let the years pass us by

So, don't you cry
Wipe the tears from your eyes

This year, you won't have to be so lonely
Don't fear, I'll be there so you can hold me
I've waited for this day to be here
I'm coming home for Christmas this year

There were many miles between us
Keeping us apart
Soon we'll be together
We'll make a brand new start
I promise you with all of my heart

We're coming into the train station now
And I know somehow
I'll never ever leave here again
I've missed my family and my friends
And I know this Christmas will bring us back together again

So, don't you cry
Wipe the tears from your eyes

This year, you won't have to be so lonely
I'm here, now you'll never have to worry
I've waited for this day to be here
I'm finally home for Christmas this year
Oh, I'm finally home for Christmas this year

I'M COMING HOME FOR CHRISTMAS
© 2004 Connor Tifarra, Connor Tifarra Entertainment

THE NEW YEAR IS HERE

© 2004 Connor Tifarra, Connor Tifarra Entertainment

It's New Years Eve once again
I'm with my family and friends
A night full of cheer
Bringing in the New Year
A night we wish never ends

The New Year is finally here
Let's give it three big cheers!
Hoooraaay! Hoooraaay! Hoooraaay!

We're all having fun because last year is done
And a new year begins today

Good tidings to all our friends
Good health and making amends
A new year of life
A future that's bright
A year to welcome new friends

The New Year is finally here
Let's give it three big cheers!
Hoooraaay! Hoooraaay! Hoooraaay!

We're all having fun because last year is done
And a new year begins today

Good tidings to all our friends

Good health and making amends
A new year of life
A future that's bright
A year to welcome new friends

The New Year is finally here
Let's give it three big cheers!
Hoooraaay! Hoooraaay! Hoooraaay!

We're all having fun because last year is done
And a new year begins today

The New Year is here!
Let's give it a cheer!
Hoooraaay!!!
A new year begins today!
Happy New Year!

THE NEW YEAR IS HERE
© 2004 Connor Tifarra, Connor Tifarra Entertainment

50 GREATEST HITS

THE CONNOR TIFARRA COLLECTION

ABOUT THE SONGS

INTRODUCTION

One of the most frequently asked questions I get as a writer is how I came up with my ideas. Songwriting is poetry. Poetry can be translated to song. I often start with words then the music and rhythm find their way to fit the mood of the story I am trying to tell. Sometimes the music comes first. You get a beat going that get's your feet tapping and the words start creating themselves from the beat and tone you have in your mind. Some of my ideas come from things I see or hear in films and television that triggers off a title or storyline. A lot of my ideas come from simply being out in the world exploring new places and seeing new faces. I see how people treat one another in loving ways or their moments of sadness and despair. It is an interesting world filled with beauty and unfortunately, some ugliness. The only ugliness is within people should they wish to let it out and the things people destroy in some way to make what once was beautiful become ugly. That gives a lot to write about. Human emotion makes story telling enjoyable to write even though the story being told may not be of a very happy subject.

A part of the writer always finds its way into the songs because each song is written from the author's point of view.

There are times when I try to write from another person's perspective such as how I think someone would feel or how they may see things. Fact of the matter is, there's no way of knowing how another person would feel or how they would see things in a certain situation. Therefore, what you are writing about is from your perspective and how you perceive them to be or how things could be. No matter what point of view you tell the story from it is still you. Be yourself and write what you would do or how you would feel even if you've never done whatever it is you are writing about or have never felt that way before. The words will have a more natural flow and the story will come together nicely.

I like all kinds of music. What I listen to depends on my mood that day. I think the mood I'm in contributes to the theme I choose to write about. The same goes for the times I am searching through stacks of notebooks with partially written songs and ideas in them. I KEEP ON TRUCKIN' as Mr. Natural would say, until I find the theme that fits my writing mood at that time. If I don't feel it I simply start a new song from scratch. Every picture tells a story and every story creates a bond between the writer and listener or reader. I enjoy the bond that can't be seen but I know exists.

To answer some of the more specific questions regarding the songs included in this songbook, I went through the songs giving insight to how or where I came up with some of the titles, lyrics or storylines and what they meant to me.

Please enjoy it!

Love Is What She Wants – I wrote this song in a dream. One night I woke remembering my dream. I grabbed a notebook and pen then began to write down what happened which included the writing of this song.

The story begins with a woman who had all her love to give and no one to give it to. She wants to be equally loved by someone but hasn't met the right person to share in that love with. I explain the woman's inner feelings of what she wants and the qualities she believes she has to offer. She hopes to meet someone that shares a similar mind set and will love her for who she is. She knows it can take some time to meet the right person. That's why she will never give up. She knows her time to be loved will soon come and dreams can come true.

Such a Beautiful Girl – When I wrote this song, I had several songs on my mind. Sammy Kershaw released a song in 1993 titled, "She Don't Know She's Beautiful." I liked the idea of writing a song about a beautiful girl so I put that right in the title. The other song I thought about was Elvis Presley's "Paralyzed" from his second album released in 1956. In Elvis' "Paralyzed," he sings of feeling hypnotized when he looked into her eyes which left him unable to speak like being paralyzed. That helped me get the word hypnotizing into the song and to describe how stunned he was at that moment. I tried a few times to get the word "perfume" into a song but couldn't get it to work with the stories I had been working on. After several attempts to add "perfume" to this song I nearly tossed the whole song right in the trash.

How he first noticed this woman when he walked into the room just wasn't working with what could have attracted him to her before their eyes met. I wanted the attraction to start from something other than the look of physical beauty that got his attention first. Just the smell of this girl's perfume made her beautiful in itself. That's how I set the stage for this attraction to take place from a distance without basing this girl's beauty on her physical looks first. This girl came to the club that night to listen to the music, dance and maybe even have fun with a little flirtation. She loved the attention but wasn't looking for love for herself.

The story leaves the reader or listener with no mention of what happened after the dancing and carrying on. Apparently, the two had a fun time, went their separate ways and he hopes he will see her again. She made such an impression on him that he was still thinking about her the next day and felt he was fortunate to have met such a beautiful girl even if it was for just one day.

We're In Love With Each Other – You just can't go wrong with a good love song. I had fun with the lyrics on this song. I wrote it as a guy singing about his girl but it could be sung by a girl singing about her guy. It's always great to write a song that could be sung by male or female. I like to have a root beer float on rainy days so I worked that into the story. I wanted a word that represented sweetness but was different from the standard comparisons. I came up with nectar. That gave me the chance to add hummingbird into the song. The music starts soft then builds towards the chorus. This brings feelings of excitement for their love as the chorus begins.

She's A Country Lady – This is a song about a city girl who dreams of being a country girl. She can't break away from her city life and job since that is her means of survival. She knows her life will probably always be this way and she will never be fully happy with it. Her only choice is to accept it at this point and to keep dreaming of what she longs for. Dreams can come true eventually if you try hard.

A Rock 'n Roll Girl – I wrote this song for country music entertainer Alan Jackson. He had a big hit in 1991 with "Don't Rock the Jukebox" and I thought this song fit his style and had that similar theme. I wanted this song to have a good solid country rock beat. I listened to Aaron Tippin's 1992 hit, "There Ain't Nothin' Wrong With The Radio" and liked the country rock feel and beat of the song. Now that I had the sound I was looking for, I had to create a story that was fun and made some kind of sense ending with a positive outcome. Here's how I pictured the story:

Have you ever been to an event where everyone is into the same thing, having a great time then someone walks in the room that you just can't help notice doesn't fit in with the current surroundings? You are in a country club with your friends listening to some good 'ol country jams. The front door slams open and in walks this Gothic looking chick with spiked blue, purple and green hair, white make-up with black lipstick, tight black vinyl pants, shirt decorated with studs around the neck, a wrist band with 2 inch steel spikes sticking out and long black boots laced up to her knees. You wonder if the zombie apocalypse happened while you were having a goodtime with your friends or if maybe you had way too much to drink. What if it turned out this girl ends up liking country music and keeps coming back? Would it matter what she wears?

Love Me – I wrote this song for country music singer Tanya Tucker. I always liked her singing style and the "Bad Girl" of country music image she portrayed. I wanted the song to be fun and sexy. I also added a fun and flirtatious breakdown clap-along with drum beat. During live performances, this is a perfect time to get the crowd on their feet and get them involved in the song.

Back to Back – I spent 2 days writing this song. I had all the music and most of the lyrics on the first day then a few lyric touch-ups the second day. The story in this song came to me while seeing a TV commercial about mattresses. The announcer was talking about sleepless nights, tossing and turning while showing two people in bed lying back to back all snugly and comfy with smiles while they slept. I took that scene and turned it into this song with a different point of view. I created my own explanation as to why the two people lay in bed back to back. Oh yeah, and they are not smiling.

Straight To Your Heart – I wrote a couple of songs for the King of Country Music, George Strait. The first one was "Straight to Your Heart." This was a war time patriotic song I wrote with a story of a soldier's duty, compassion and hope. This song has a strong message and I thought George would be perfect for this type of song. I also thought another bonus to the song's title was the opportunity to use it for an album title.

Next was "**Sometimes You Win, Sometimes You Lose.**" I wrote this song about encouragement, never giving up on your dreams and knowing you will probably take a couple falls on your way to success. This song is pretty straight forward with a great a cappella opening and solo vocal ending. "**Key To My Heart**" is a fun song all the way around. I made sure this song had a beat that you just couldn't help but move some part of your body to. It's witty, catchy and makes you want to hear more!

Rollin' On Down The Line – One night I was visiting with a few friends talking about music and a new song I had a rough draft on. I picked up a guitar and belted out this song. They loved it! It's another one of those songs you just can't get enough of because the music is fun and makes you feel good.

They Call Me a Rebel – I wrote this song in 2005 for Evel Knievel and all motorcycle riders of the world to have a nice cruisin' song. I used Harley-Davidson as reference in the song because of their quality, reliability and popularity. I was happy to make reference to Evel Knievel in the song and did that by using EK Loop (Evel Knievel Loop) which is a 6 mile cruise spot in Evel's home town of Butte, Montana. My favorite quote by Evel Knievel is, "*Dying is a part of living and none of us are going to get out of here alive.*" Evel died November 30, 2007.

40 Long Days – I love trucker music both older and newer. If the song is about truckin' or semi's I like it! I have an extensive collection of trucker related songs by artists such as Red Sovine, Red Simpson, Del Reeves, Dave Dudley,

Junior Brown and Jerry Reed just to name a few. I decided to give it a go at writing a trucker song and this is it. I like songs with a fun beat while I'm driving to pass the miles by with. I made this a feel good driving song with a fun up-beat tempo.

It's Been A Good Life – I was listening to some songs by Eddie Rabbitt when I wrote this. His style and song rhythms gave me ideas to fit the mood and message I was thinking about at the time. A guy takes a trip around the world and meets a girl he falls in love with in another country. They marry, have a family and have had a great life together. He shares a little about their meeting, the reasons for his happiness and how thankful he is for all the years she stuck with him through everything.

I Tripped And Fell In Love – My idea for the title of this song came from an Elvis Presley 1961 hit, "I Slipped, I Stumbled, I Fell." I played with the words and got a clever title out of it. The style and overall tone of this song came to me while listening to some great music by Jim Croce and his guitar player Maury Muehleisen. I wrote this song to fit Jim's similar singing fashion and storytelling.

Yesterday Was a Damn Good Day – Hank Williams Jr. once told me to, "Hang in there. Never give up on your dream and to keep writing!" I was thinking about him when I came up with the story and mood on the song. Hank is a fantastic writer and entertainer. He's great at story telling songs. "The Blues Man" from 1980 and "A Country Boy Can Survive" from 1981 came to mind which had me thinking of the mood I wanted to set and the spoken yet, almost singing telling of the story. I kept that flow throughout the verses and gave the somewhat, singing part to the chorus.

Broken Promises – I got the title and story for this song while I was watching an episode of The Jerry Springer Show. Jerry brought out a male guest and talked with him about how the guy screwed up his life by cheating on his wife and making her life as miserable as possible. This theme was pretty typical on Jerry Springer's show. Then Jerry brought out the wife who was listening the whole time from backstage. She comes out breathing fire from her nostrils, stomping, screaming and waving her finger in the husbands face. She screams, "You're a piece of crap! You promised me a better life and broke every promise you ever made! You said everything would be alright and look where that got us, on The Jerry Springer Show!" Right then, I had the title and the first words to begin the story.
The wife said that all they do is fight and she couldn't go on living with him this way so she was leaving him. The rest of the couple's interview with Jerry helped me find the words I needed to tell the whole story.

I tell of the love they once had, what tore their love apart and what she was going to do about it knowing their broken love could not be glued back together. Even if she had faith things could work out after the pieces of their relationship were glued back in place, there would still be the cracks left behind from the damage that had already been done. A broken vase that's been glued back together will eventually break apart again and will be thrown into the trash only existing as a memory just like the relationship of these two people.

The moral of the story is, sometimes you can't fix what is broken and it may be best to let it go and exist only as a memory. Eventually the memory will fade away and in the end, will die with you.

Nothing Lasts – If you don't jump on an opportunity when one comes up you might not get a second chance to make it happen. When you see someone you would like to meet the same rule may apply. Don't be shy and waste the time away. Happiness may be just around the corner if you build up some guts and simply go for it.

Let's Fly Away – My original title for this song was simply, "Mars." My plan was to write about the planet Mars and humans obsession with it. I thought it might make a good heavy metal thrash tune or something like Queensryche's, "Silent Lucidity." I just couldn't keep a good storyline going or get the right sound I wanted. I also ran out of things to say about the planet that could keep the story interesting. I took pieces of the lyrics I had and turned it into a love song. I guess I was in a mellow mood that day and that's why the rockin' tune didn't work. I just didn't feel it. Writing about Mars was scrapped but I still wanted to get the word Mars into the song. I used the word Mars once in the whole thing.

Two Young Lovers – People are always trying to tell other people what they should and shouldn't do, who they can love, hang around and the likes thereof. That's what this song is about. No one has the right to tell you a damn thing about anything you do whether anyone else likes it or not. You have a right to be happy.

Next Time You're Lonely – Sometimes it's nice to be alone. Sometimes it stinks on ice. It's nice to know there's always a good friend close by for the good times and the sad times as well. I wrote this song in a way that tells the listener or reader that there are a lot of people that share in similar feelings as they do. You don't have to be poor to be lonely. You don't have to be rich to be lonely. You can be standing in a group of one hundred people and you can be lonely.

Watching The Wagon Wheel Roll 'Round – For the story of this song I thought about an old man sitting by an outdoor fire telling a group of friends about a significant time in his life. That time was the day his family took their horses and covered wagon across the country to California in search for a better life. It was a long, hard trip with triumphs and tragedies. His family's strength and determination prevailed and they made it to their destination. This experience taught him to be a survivor. It is his strength and determination that helped him continue living and to become an old man. This is his story of a family's dreams, courage, love, tragedy and hope for their future.

The Brave – From the late 1980's to the early 2000's, quite a few patriotic songs came out to support troops in Iraq and their families during the Saddam Hussein years and into Afghanistan. This was a big business opportunity for the music publishing and recording industries. Songs about tragedy and hope always brings big dollars especially during times of turmoil, conflict and loss. I wrote this song during that timeframe because it was trendy. "**Straight To Your Heart**" was another patriotic song I penned during this time.

Rainy Day Girl & You're My Rainy Day Girl – I wanted to write a song that I could write an answer song to. It's been done a few times throughout music history with a few reaching pretty good sales and popularity. This was my first attempt to write a song while trying to make the story flow in a way that could make sense if someone sang the same song from their own personal point of view. Not as an answer song but as a companion song. Using *The Connor Tifarra Reverse Lyric Method*, I wrote "Rainy Day Girl" for Beyonce' and "You're My Rainy Day Girl" for a male vocalist as the companion or "Reverse Lyric" song. I thought the words and sexy feel to "Rainy Day Girl" was just right for Beyonce's style, image and fan base. Working towards the end of the song I wanted the listener to be excited for her and to feel this girl's happiness with her. To share in her feelings of rainbows after the rain and walking on air with love abound! A happy ending makes a positive ending. I used the same method for "You're My Rainy Day Girl," keeping the same flow of happiness continuing through fadeout.

21 Lovers Lane – The disease known as Cancer takes away many lives every day. This is the story of a young couple in love and how their lives were separated by one of them dying from Cancer. 21 was the girl's age when she died.
The one left living shares the memory of their love and their tragedy.

Letting Go of Love – I think a lot of people have had to let go of love some way or another and to have to do it isn't always easy. Maybe it never is. I wrote this song trying to share with the listener or reader a story of common everyday life. The story may not have the same reasons for the loss of love for each person, though the story tells of a common experience we most likely share. It's always fun to write a song about a feeling or event that the writer and listeners or readers can relate to. This is the kind of song that builds the writer and listener bond.

Roses, Rainbows and You – I wrote this song for music legend Willie Nelson. Willie's road crew is fantastic and I always have a great time with them. This song tells the story of the love this person once embraced but now has no one to hold. All this person has left is the garden that still grows and the memory of what once was. Some people have a hard time when it comes to letting go of what used-to-be and are afraid to move on. They dwell on the past and refuse to continue living in the now and for the future. They tend to trap themselves in a time from the past thinking life will be easier if they pretend a dead loved one is still there by fantasizing about them as if they were still there. It's a nice thought and might make you feel better for a while but, you have to get out what you feel about your loss and start living again.

Looking At The Outside – Most people have probably heard the saying, "Never judge a book by its cover." That's what gave me the idea for this tune. I think that statement is true most of the time but not always. I decided to write the song from a relationship point of view. It's pretty tough for love to grow if you never take the time to "really" learn about each other for more than the physical aspects that may have first attracted you to one another. Try taking the time to look at the inside before you run away. You might learn a lot for better or for worse.

Holly – The day I started writing this song I hadn't yet come up with the name I wanted to use in it. Later that day I visited a friend named Holly and decided to use her name for my story. Sometimes just a change of scenery and atmosphere can bring new ideas. That's how things worked out on this day.

Time Plays The Game – I wrote this song for Roger Daltry of the rock band The Who. The song starts and ends with a familiar, "Who" sound with a lot of Pink Floyd influence throughout the tone of the music and flow of words. This song has a few change-ups that flows from one song to another and back again. This effect gives the listener a more album rock style song and uses of several instrumental breaks.

Trapped – I wrote a few songs for Matchbox Twenty. I like the writing style of Rob Thomas and his use of words to describe the emotional aspect in his songs. Rob wants the listener to feel what he feels. He does this by stating the current emotion he is experiencing at that moment in the song. He may be daydreaming and fantasizing or hurt and crying, etc... I express as much emotion as I can based on what theme I am writing about. Emotion is important in song and perhaps even more so in non-musical poetry.

The songs **"Trapped," "Turn My Life Around," "Delusions," "I'm Feeling Down," "I'll Have to Dream Alone"** and **"The Decision"** are all part of the emotional journey songs I wrote. Each of the songs, share a similar theme and purpose. The six songs together tell the story.

Exit 41 – I didn't plan on this song being about playing billiards when I first thought to write it. I intended this story being about a party going on at Exit 41 off the highway.
I ended up making Exit 41 the name of the pool hall the guy likes to play at instead. The guy in the story is a pool hustler that get's hustled by a hot girl in tight pants.
Since the song turned out to be about billiards I tossed in reference to a couple legendary pool players stating even the greatest of the game couldn't beat this girl. Most likely they lose because they can't keep their eyes off her T&A.

Invisible – I wrote this song in 2 hours 26 minutes. Some songs have literally taken me years to complete because I sometimes get one started then lose the feel and set it aside. I shuffle through them now and then looking for the one that screams out to be finished. I was thinking about how some relationships start out exciting giving one another all kinds of attention. As time goes by, some people become distant from each other and turn into near or complete avoidance. They stop talking, pretend they are busy with something or just say, "uh huh, uh huh, yeah." They treat you like you're not there or they wish you weren't there at all.
I have personally experienced this type of scenario on many occasions. It's typical of many relationships especially in the 21st Century where no one takes the time for anyone but themselves. It's selfish, rude and disgusting. This song is what I think about it.

Expensive Bitch – My idea for this song came from witnessing such situations out in the world. Some people do these things to people and some people are victims of it or actually enjoy that kind of relationship. These people are the users and the used. It was an interesting subject to write about. Some songs by the Steve Miller Band influenced me on the musical sound I was looking for.

All My Life – I thought about writing a song with loud bells being struck with a deep drum hitting in unison. BAM! BAM! BAM! It stuck in my head and was coming out as a thrash or heavy metal song. I didn't really care for it myself at first but I couldn't get it out of my thoughts. So, I wrote it to let it out of my system. I thought about a couple songs that used a striking bell which were "Tubular Bells" by Mike Oldfield in 1973 and "Hell's Bell's" by AC/DC from 1980. I wanted this song to have a unique element to it. Something you wouldn't expect to hear in a thrash type of song. After trying a few different instruments to use for a solo break, I decided on adding a ukulele with a mellow singing voice. This change-up is sung with feeling and then returning to the striking bells and drum. This leads right back into the thrashing chorus with a single bell strike to fade ending which leads into the next song. It worked out great.

Heart of Fire – Most people are so one-way minded they will interpret this song as referring to Satan the first time they read or hear it. Maybe it is, maybe it isn't. Maybe it's about the leader of a nation and the leaders of the military which are both powers of evil in themselves. Perhaps they are one in the same. Whatever interpretation comes to your mind still works for the song regardless. All I know is that this song jams!

TIC-TAC-DIE – Ah! The beauty of power, corruption and war! ***STOP KILLING EACH OTHER!***

Undercover Lies – I originally wrote this rockin' tune as a poem. I changed the structure a bit then added a chorus and change-up. Some of the references in the song I wrote as I see the Government and some came from experiencing it. I was watching a movie called "The Edge" starring Anthony Hopkins and Alec Baldwin that came out in 1997. While I was working on the song I re-arranged a line from the film which was said buy Hopkins character, "Never feel sorry for a man with a plane" and re-wrote the line to, "Don't trust a man with a plane." I thought about how the Grizzly bear (who's actual name was Bart) was stalking the men that were already wounded and weak from crashing their plane into the lake. The three survivors started walking through the woods trying to find their way back to the lodge where they were staying. The bear would secretly follow them, watch their every move, study their vulnerabilities and wait for the precise moment to strike with full force. Similar to how the Government and underground Mafia hit-men operate. The bear, like the Mafia Boys and Government (what's the difference?) wait until a person is weak and vulnerable then make their attack. Buddy Ebsen who played Jed Clampet on the 1960's TV series The Beverly Hillbillies, received a quick reference from me by using the line, "Jed, he's a millionaire," which was said in the opening theme song. This reference is in regards to the money makers of the underground movement that do exist in secret and are everywhere right in front of our face. Most people don't see it or they are just too ignorant and closed minded to believe it.

The American Dream – This is one of my famous sarcastic style songs. Every once in a while I like to write a song that get's people thinking. Maybe thinking about what

kind of person they are and what their purpose in life is. If you are offended by this song and what it implies then you must be the kind of person I'm writing about and you help prove my point.
This song is how I see Americans and people all over the globe for that matter. It's one of those like it or hate it songs. Writing a good controversial song always brings attention to you and that means publicity which in turn brings MONEY! If you are one of the people that can't stand this song and it makes you angry, go tell everyone you can. Help promote me and the song as much as you can. Same thing if you love it! I win both ways.

Defenestration – Suicide is a sad thing. People find all kinds of inventive ways to accomplish their goal. This song is about what I think about the jumpers. Neil Armstrong took a giant leap for mankind and Van Halen sang to, "Go ahead and jump." You might as well.

Countdown Clock – TICK, TOCK, TICK, TOCK, goes your countdown clock. Time is counting down for you to not be around. When your clock stops you go 6 feet down. Unless of course you enjoy the thought of your body sliding into a cremation chamber getting fried with flames until your just a little pile of bone fragments and ashes. Either way you choose your toast. Do you need to borrow a stick of butter and some of those little jelly packets?

Better Go Get Her – This song started out as an instrumental jam I wrote for promotional purposes. 30 second clips were used to attract consumers. I really liked the music and wanted to give it some words. I added some peanut butter to the jam and gave the music a story to tell. The instrumental version and lyric version worked out nice both ways.

I'm Coming Home For Christmas – I only wrote a couple Christmas songs. There's really no market for it anymore. Everyone still likes the old traditional Holiday songs that sing about wishing people a Merry Christmas and bringing them some figgy pudding. I don't know if writing about figgy pudding could ever be topped but I gave it my best shot.

The New Year Is Here – Is there any other New Years song in existence other than Auld Lang Syne? There is NOW!

50 GREATEST HITS

THE CONNOR TIFARRA COLLECTION

Connor Tifarra Entertainment

www.ingramcontent.com/pod-product-compliance
Lightning Source LLC
Chambersburg PA
CBHW061650040426
42446CB00010B/1673